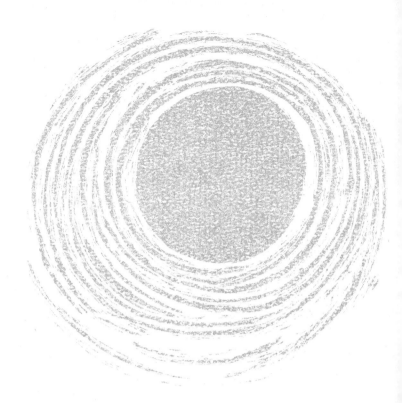

# Together We Walk

### by Peter S. Seymour
### Illustrated by
### Pamela Brunke

♛ HALLMARK CROWN EDITIONS

Together we walk.....

friends in our sameness...in our differences....
in sunshine and rain...

through field and forest....

across mountain and river...giving....

sharing...in simplicity and trust....

together in the journey of living....

Together like two leaves

spinning down a crystal stream....

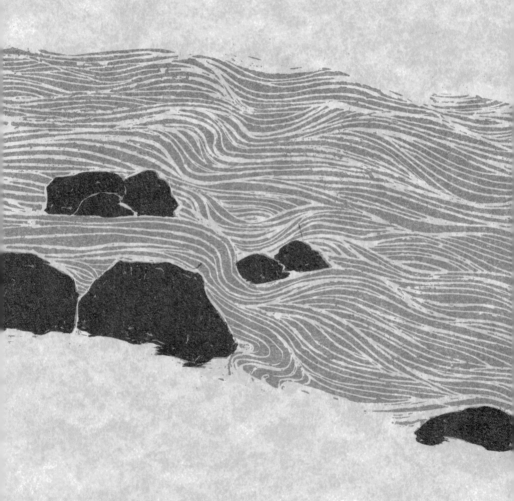

Together like a giant oak
    towering beside gold-waving grasses,
or ivy twining around a low granite rock.

As we walk, friends laughing in sunshine,
we are playful as fawns
on the pine needles....

We run with the clouds scudding across

the sapphire sky....

....we laugh with the dancing surf...

We stand prim and proper,

like two ladybugs on a single leaf.

Friends...together...trusting

as the birds trust the wind....

....as the plants rely on the trinity
of earth, raindrops, and sun.

We comfort each other in the storm...
sheltering as a mantle of boughs shelters
the robin's nest.

Together we ramble...friends....

open as the fields and valleys,

sharing our green joy....

....or dreamy in the silences of shadows,

lost in the myriad lights

of mottled leaves

in the forest noon....

returning the sea to the sand....

....sometimes

reflecting each other's thoughts,

like the mystic mosaics

of a mountain lake....

Together we go, certain as the tide

....tender

  as the horizon

    cradling the dawn

and singing the sun to sleep.

Together...yet individual....

    merging our uniqueness...as the scents

of orange blossoms

    blend with wild dill and mint

        by the trail....

....all mingling in one fresh breeze....

in the delicious fragrance....

in the wondrous sense

of one eternal source

for all togetherness.

And though the path divides....

and sometimes we must move

in and out of different doorways

of the world....

and cross other vistas of experience....

....still we are together,
in the heart of things....
patient as seedlings....
    till we bloom again
        along the same
flourishing byway.

I
love
you,
Sam

Then together we walk onward....

beyond our vision....

into the unknown....

where the path may be

steep or narrow....

wide or straight....

in sunshine and rain....

It matters not,

because we are secure....

and move toward greater wisdom....

blending in the glory of life....

.........and the promise of tomorrow.........

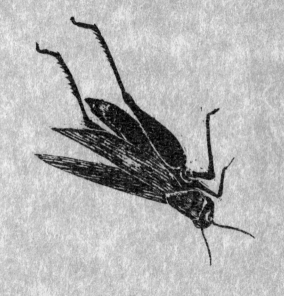

This book was designed and illustrated by Pamela Brunke.
The artist made her own color separations
and closely supervised the printing for utmost accuracy
of reproduction. The type is set in Shakespeare,
a roman typeface designed by Gudrun Zapf von Hesse
exclusively for Hallmark Editions. The paper is Halltclear.
White Imitation Parchment and Ivory Fiesta Parchment.
The cover is bound with imported natural Seta silk
book cloth and Torino paper.